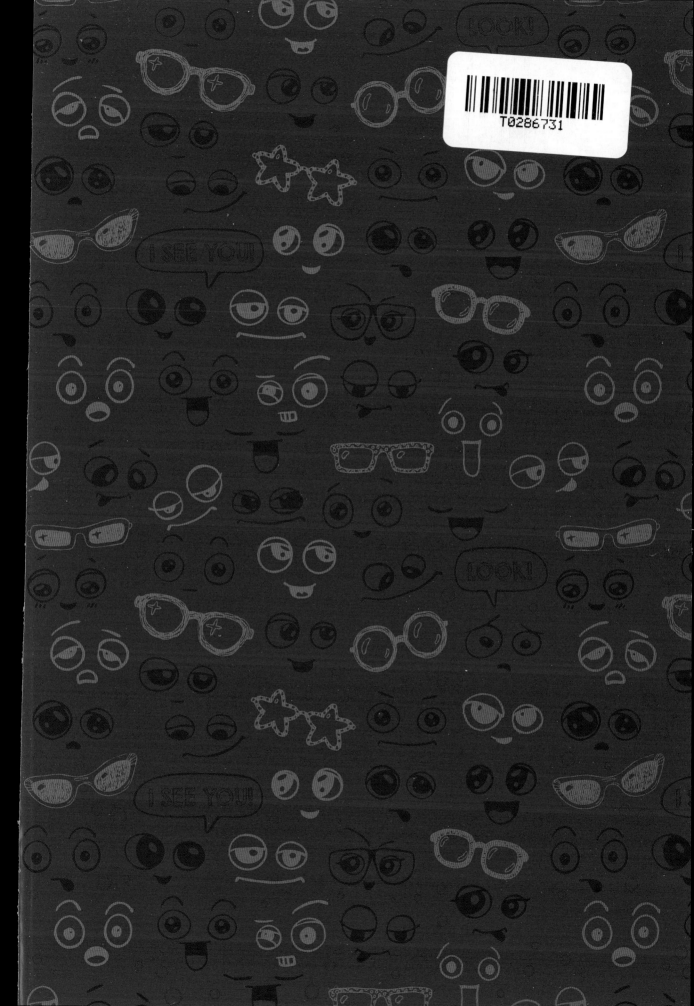

My Sense of
SIGHT

Ellen Lawrence

sequoia™
kids media

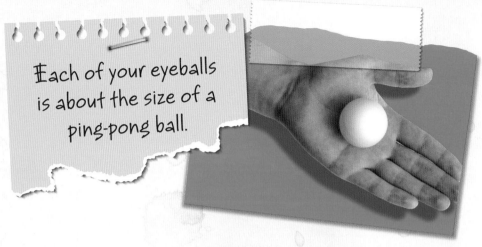

Each of your eyeballs is about the size of a ping-pong ball.

Consultant:
Suzy Gazlay, MA
Recipient, Presidential Award for Excellence in Science Teaching

Photography © Shutterstock 2023 123Done; Aleks Melnik; alexandre zveiger; Anatoliy Karlyuk; Andrei Kuzmik; Ania Samoilova; Barks; bluelela; Djem; Dovina; Drawlab19; Dzm1try; Federico Rostagno; frozenbunn; Gelpi; Goodreason; Hardtlllustrations; hchjjl; In Green; Iren_Geo; Iryna Dobrovynska; Javier Brosch; karelnoppe; Kiselev Andrey Valerevich; KK Tan; Krakenimages.com; krugloff; LHF Graphics; LightField Studios; LintangDesign; memej; mhatzapa; mijatmijatovic; Nataliya Hora; Nerthuz; Nik Merkulov; Nikolaeva; paranormal; Paul Orr; Polar_lights15; prochasson frederic; Prostock-studio; Roman Chazov; Roman Malyshev; Roman Samborskyi; Ruslan Shugushev; sonya etchison; Studio Romantic; suerz; SUKJAI PHOTO; Tartila; wavebreakmedia; Zapatosoldador
Additional photography provided by Ruby Tuesday Books (pp. 6-7, 11, 17)

Published by Sequoia Kids Media,
an imprint of Sequoia Publishing & Media, LLC

Sequoia Publishing & Media, LLC,
a division of Phoenix International Publications, Inc.

8501 West Higgins Road
Chicago, Illinois 60631

© 2024 Sequoia Publishing & Media, LLC
First published © Ruby Tuesday Books Limited

CustomerService@PhoenixInternational.com

I can see the words now!

I have blue eyes!

www.SequoiaKidsMedia.com

Library of Congress Control Number: 2023935266

ISBN: 979-8-7654-0298-6

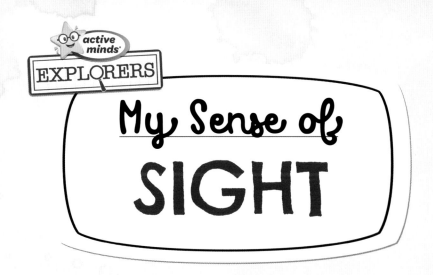

active minds EXPLORERS

My Sense of SIGHT

Table of Contents

Seeing Your World...4

Light in Your World............................... 6

Check Out Your Eyes................................8

What's Inside Your Eyeball?......................10

Making Pictures.......................................12

Your Brain Gets Busy..............................14

Amazing Eyeballs 16

Help with Seeing......................................18

Take Care of Your Eyes........................... 20

Glossary.. 22

Index 24

Read More 24

Visit Us...24

Words shown in **bold** in the text are explained in the glossary.

I SEE IT!

Seeing Your World

From the moment you open your eyes in the morning, you see the world around you.

Your **sense** of sight helps you get dressed, play sports, read books, and see your friends.

It keeps you safe by letting you look for cars as you cross the street.

You can even see your own face when you look in a mirror.

Each day your eyes see thousands of colors, shapes, and movements.

Just how does this amazing sense work, though? Let's find out!

Your body has five senses. These are seeing, hearing, smelling, tasting, and touching. Your senses help keep you safe. They also help you enjoy the world around you.

I SEE IT!

Light in Your World

In order to see the world around us, we need light.

In the daytime, light usually comes from the sun.

At night, we switch on lamps and other types of lighting.

When light from the sun or a lamp hits an object, the light bounces or reflects off the object.

Your eyes capture this reflected light.

If you stand in a completely dark room, you can't see the objects around you. That's because there is no light reflecting off the objects. Your eyes are still working, but there is no light for your eyes to capture.

Then your eyes and brain work together to allow you to see the object.

The sun

1 Light hits the sunflowers.

2 The sunflowers reflect the light.

3 Your eyes capture the reflected light, and you see the sunflowers.

Check Out Your Eyes

Without your eyes, or eyeballs, you wouldn't be able to see everything that's going on around you.

Your eyeballs are safely tucked inside your head, so you can only see a small part of them.

The white part of your eye that you can see is a tough, outer covering called the **sclera**.

The round, colored part of your eyeball is called the **iris**.

In the center of your iris is a **pupil**.

Each of your eyeballs is about the size of a ping-pong ball.

Your pupil looks black, but it's actually a small, round opening with an important job to do.

The irises of a person's eyes can be brown, green, or blue.

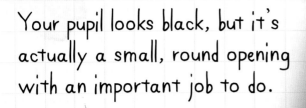

Sclera

Iris   Pupil

I have blue eyes!

Every time you blink, your eyelids clean your eyes and **moisten** them. If you didn't blink, your eyes would get dirty and dry.

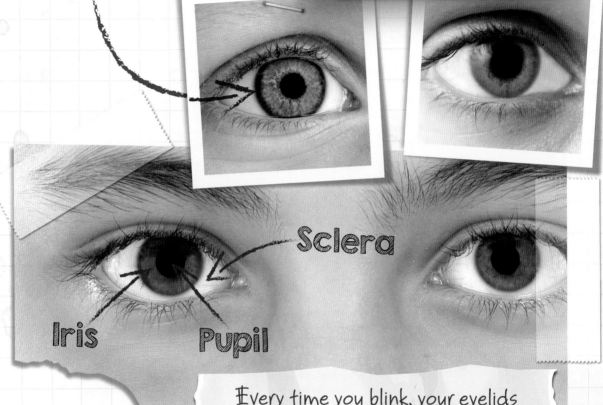

Eyelid

You can make yourself blink, but your eyelids also blink without you even thinking about it.

What's Inside Your Eyeball?

Each of your eyes is covered with a see-through, dome-shaped layer of **tissue** called the **cornea**.

The cornea captures light and directs it into your eye through your pupil.

Once the light is inside your eye, it hits another see-through part called the **lens**.

It's too bright!

Tiny muscles in your irises can make your pupils get bigger or smaller. If light is very bright, your pupils get smaller. This stops too much light from entering your eyes.

The job of your lens is to focus light onto the back of your eyeball.

This back part of your eye is called the **retina**.

If there is not enough light, your pupils get bigger. This lets as much light into your eyes as possible.

Small pupil

Big pupil

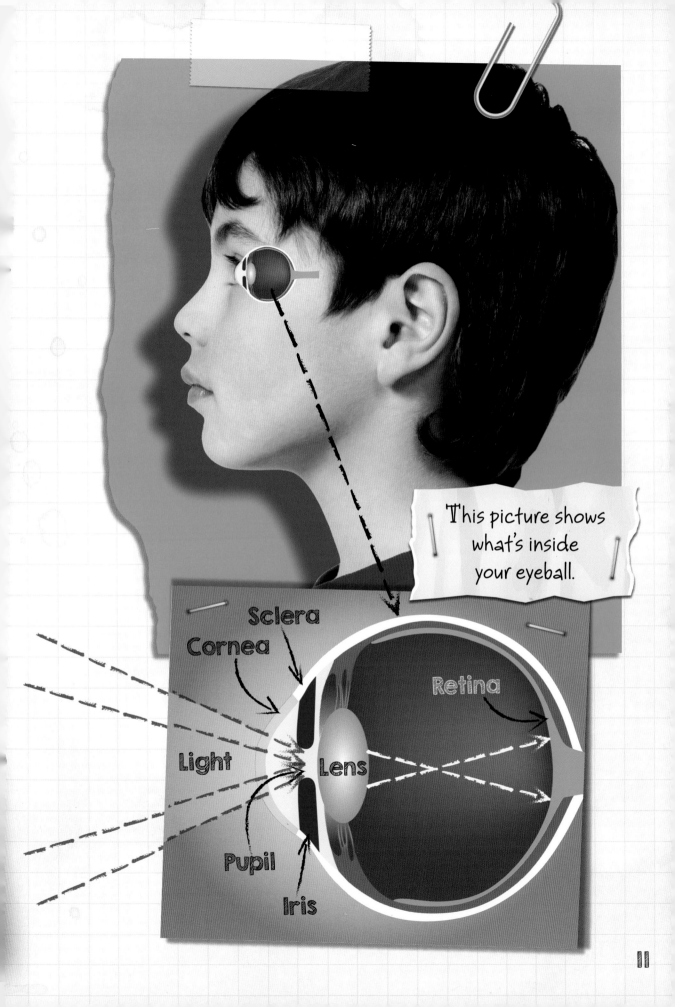

This picture shows what's inside your eyeball.

Sclera

Cornea

Retina

Light

Lens

Pupil

Iris

Making Pictures

Each of your retinas contains millions of tiny **cells** called **rods** and **cones**.

The light that your eye has captured hits these cells.

The hardworking rods and cones collect lots of information from the light.

I'm right side up!!

The picture created by your retina is actually upside down!

Then they use the information to create a picture.

The picture is sent as messages along your **optic nerve** to your brain.

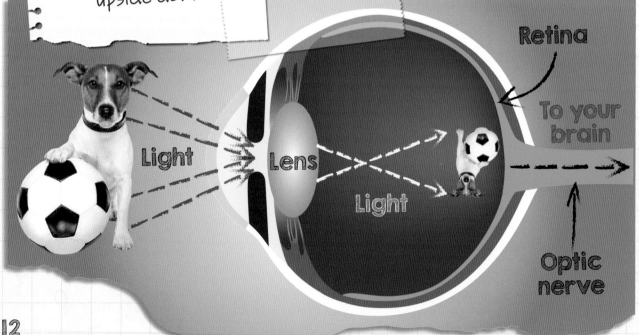

Retina

To your brain

Light

Lens

Light

Optic nerve

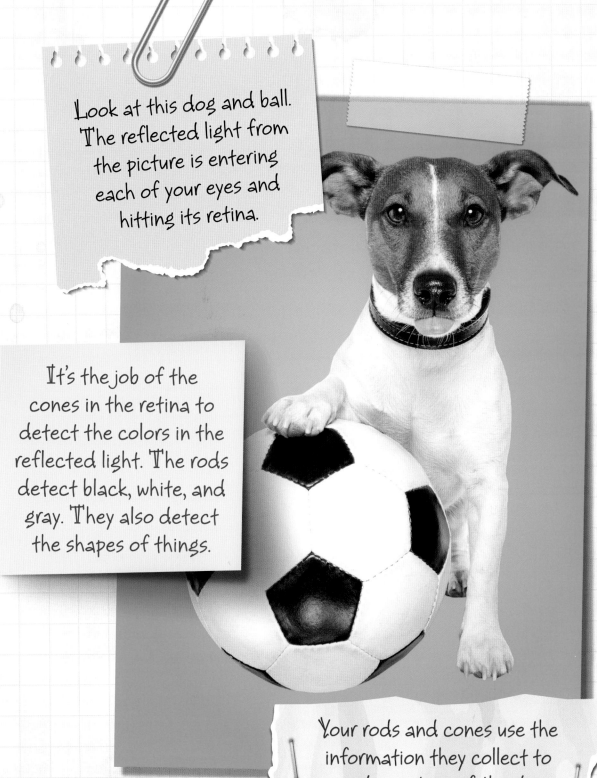

Look at this dog and ball. The reflected light from the picture is entering each of your eyes and hitting its retina.

It's the job of the cones in the retina to detect the colors in the reflected light. The rods detect black, white, and gray. They also detect the shapes of things.

Your rods and cones use the information they collect to send a picture of the dog and ball to your brain.

Each of your retinas contains about 120 million rods and 7 million cones!

Your Brain Gets Busy

The upside-down picture created by your retina speeds along your optic nerve.

When your brain receives the picture, it flips it the right way up.

Then, your brain figures out what the picture shows.

In an instant, you see the object you were looking at!

Your amazing eyes and brain help you see shapes, movements, and about 10 million different colors!

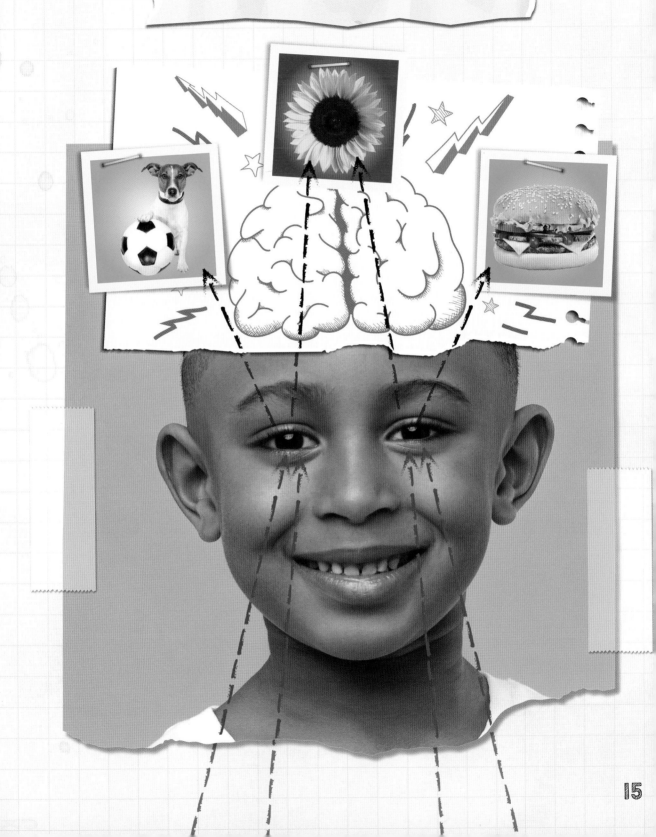

Every second your eyes are open, pictures of your world are zooming from your eyes to your brain.

Amazing Eyeballs

Look up. Look down. Look at something far away or something that's near to you.

Your busy eyes have lots of ways to make sure you see everything around you.

To do their job, the lenses in your eyes can actually change shape.

To make sure you can see objects that are very near to you, your lenses get thicker.

When you want to look at something that's far away, your lenses get thinner.

Each of your eyeballs has six tiny muscles attached to it. The muscles help you move your eyes up and down and side to side.

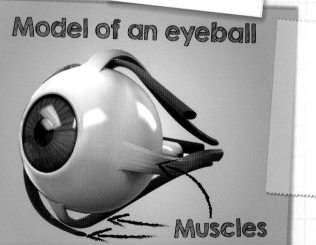

Model of an eyeball

Muscles

When you look at the dog that's near to you, this is what you see.

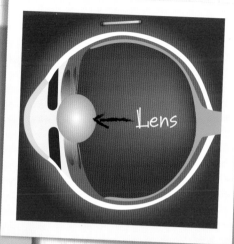

The lenses in your eyes get thicker.

When you look at the sunflowers that are far away, this is what you see.

The lenses in your eyes get thinner.

Help with Seeing

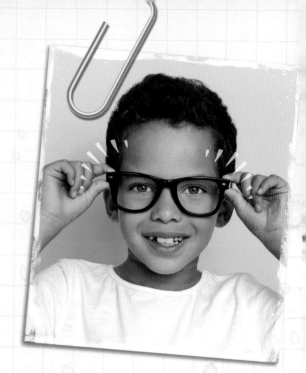

Not everyone sees in the same way.

Some people can't see things clearly that are far away.

I can see the words now!

Others can see things in the distance, but have trouble seeing things that are up close.

These differences in sight can happen if parts of a person's eyes are not doing their jobs.

The lenses in our eyes may not focus light onto our retinas properly. This means that pictures created by the retinas are fuzzy. Wearing glasses or contact lenses helps fix this.

Usually, it's possible for people to wear glasses or **contact lenses** to improve how they see.

Often people's eyes don't see as well as they get older. Think of all the adults you know. How many of them wear glasses?

Some people are blind and have a guide dog. A guide dog is trained to keep its owner safe. Guide dogs can help their owners cross the street and lead them onto buses and trains.

A guide dog

Take Care of Your Eyes

All day, every day, your eyes are keeping you safe and helping you have fun.

In fact, your sense of sight is the busiest of all your senses.

It's very important, therefore, that you take good care of your eyes.

If you play sports such as football or hockey, you can wear a helmet with a shield to protect your eyes.

On sunny days, wear sunglasses to protect your eyes from bright sunlight.

Taking good care of your amazing eyes will help them keep on taking care of you!

If you watch TV or look at your phone or a computer for too long, it will make your eyes tired. Every 20 to 30 minutes, try to give your eyes a rest and spend some time away from the screen.

If your eyes hurt or feel tired, tell a grown-up. Also, tell your teacher if you're having trouble seeing the board at school, or seeing the words in your books. Then you can arrange to see an eye doctor and get an eye check-up.

Glossary

cells (SELZ)
Very tiny parts of a living thing. Your bones, muscles, skin, hair, and every part of you are made of cells.

cones (KOHNZ)
Cells in your retinas that detect colors in the light that enters your eyes.

contact lenses (KON-takt LEN-ziz)

Small, see-through disks that some people wear on their eyes to help improve their sight. Contact lenses are placed onto a person's corneas.

cornea (KOR-nee-uh)
A see-through, dome-shaped layer of tissue that covers your iris and pupil. The cornea captures light and directs it into your eye.

iris (EYE-riss)
The colored, circular part of your eye.

lens (LENZ)
A see-through part of your eye that focuses light onto the retina.

moisten (MOI-suhn)
Make something slightly wet.

optic nerve (OP-tik NURV)
A group of cells that carry information from the retina in your eye to your brain.

pupil (PYOO-puhl)
A small, round opening in the center of your eye. The pupil looks black, but it's actually a small hole that allows light to enter your eye.

retina (RET-in-uh)
The back wall of your eyeball. Cells, called rods and cones, in your retinas take the light that enters your eyes and help turn it into the things you see.

rods (RODZ)
Cells in your retinas that detect shapes in the light that enters your eyes. Rods also detect black, white, and gray.

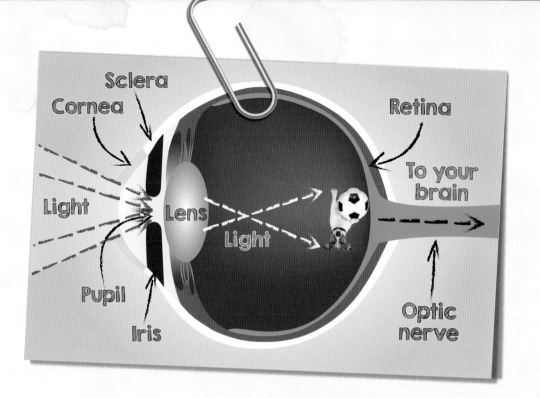

sclera (SKLER-uh)
The white part of your eye. The sclera is a tough, outer covering for the eyeball.

sense (SENSS)
One of the five ways that you collect information about the world around you. Your senses are seeing, hearing, smelling, tasting, and touching.

tissue (TISH-yoo)
A group of connected cells in your body that work together. Cells are very tiny parts of a living thing. Skin tissue, for example, is made up of skin cells.

Index

B
blindness 19
blinking 9
brain 6, 12–13, 14–15

C
caring for eyes 20–21
cells 12
colors 4, 13, 14
cones 12–13
contact lenses 18
corneas 10–11

D
doctors 21

E
eyelids 9
eyes 4, 6–7, 8–9, 10–11,
  12–13, 14–15, 16–17,
  18–19, 20–21

G
glasses 18–19
guide dogs 19

I
irises 8–9, 10–11

L
lenses 10–11, 12, 16–17, 18
light 6–7, 10–11, 12–13, 18

M
movements 4, 14
muscles 10, 16

O
optic nerves 12, 14

P
pupils 8–9, 10–11

R
reflected light 6–7, 13
retinas 10–11, 12–13,
  14, 18
rods 12–13

S
sclera 8–9, 11
senses 4–5, 20
shapes 4, 13, 14
sun, the 6–7, 20
sunglasses 20

Read More

My Little Book about Me
Angela Royston
London: Quarto Library (2022).

A Journey Through the Human Body
Steve Parker
Beverly, MA: Quarto Library (2022).

Visit Us

www.SequoiaKidsMedia.com
Downloadable content and more!

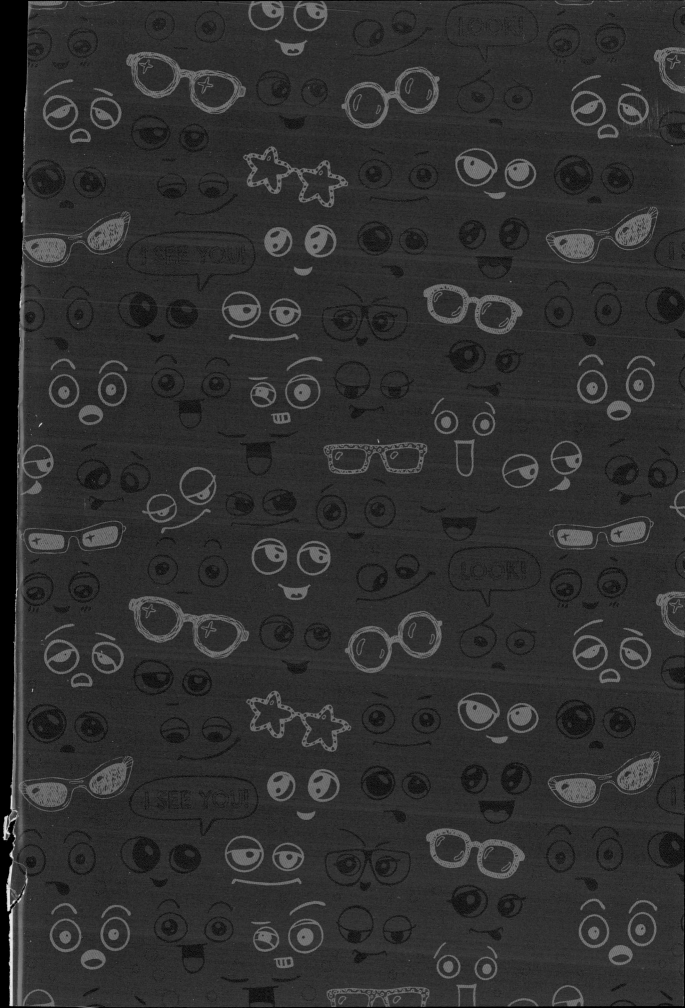

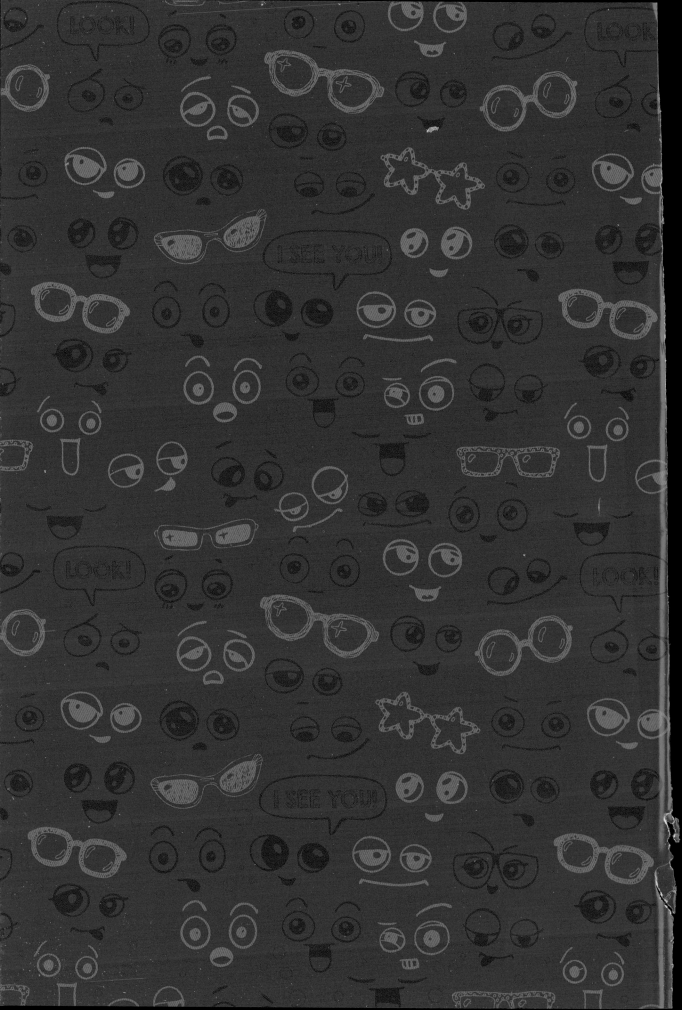